How to go Viral in The Marketing World

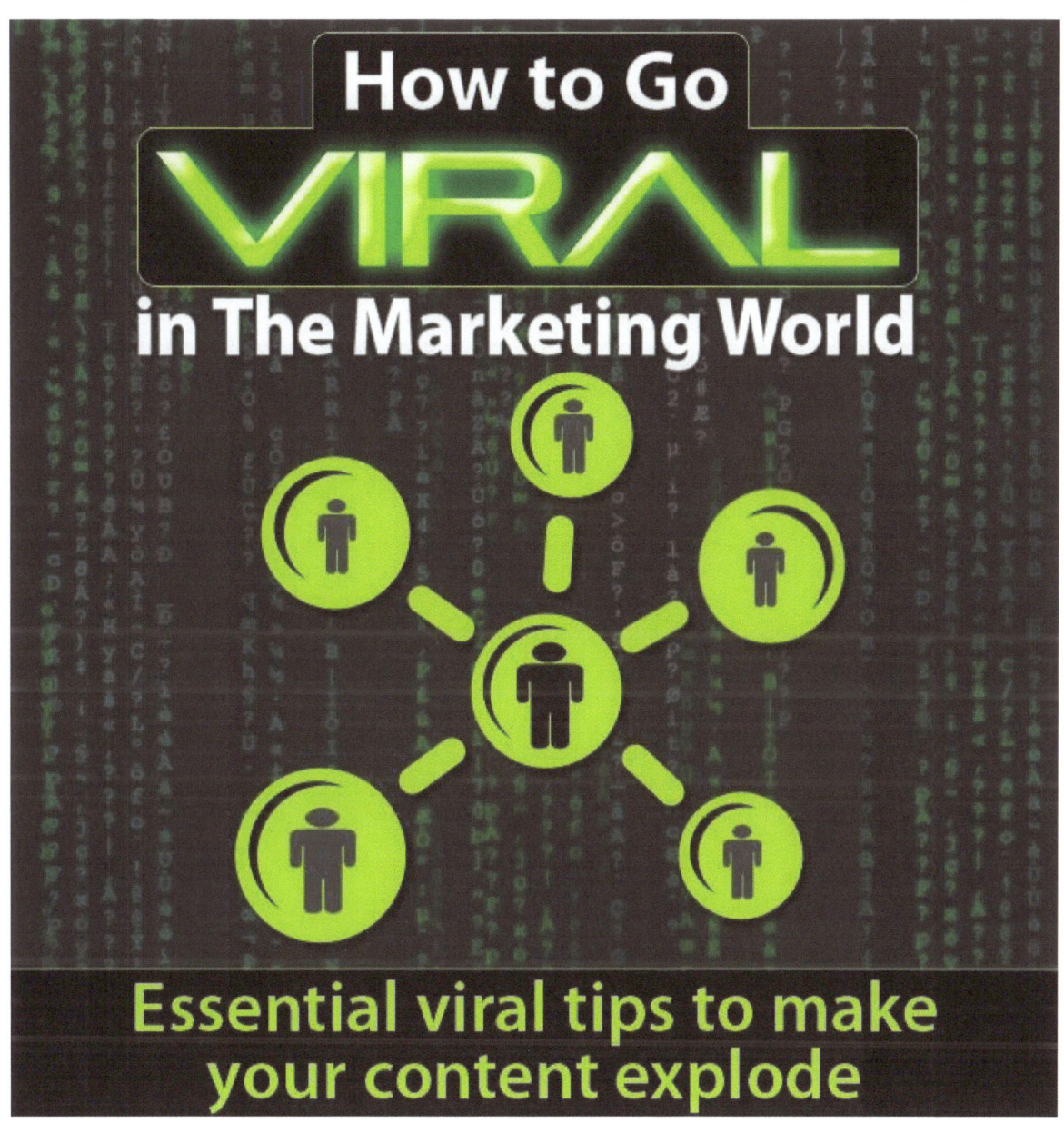

Contents

About The Viral Buzz

Viral marketing buzz occurs daily, in normal, unspectacular circumstances and when you least anticipate it.

The grapevine, rumours, the whispers in your ear are what buzz is all about. Those little flecks of information that individuals share over a cup of java….the outrageous occurrence that somebody just saw and can't wait to describe or the unbelievably cool product that a acquaintance of a friend just purchased are the body and soul of buzz…and buzz marketing or viral marketing, depending upon what you wish to call it.

We all recognize what a computer virus is. It spreads from one PC to another in the blink of an eye. Now "Buzz" is the virus of promoting… it spreads to other buyers and has an epidemic of sales of your product or service.

It may be that "e-mail this to an acquaintance" button that's simply calling to you to click it, or a pair of real (and really satisfied) lips whispering persuasive endorsements into receptive ears; buzz marketing may transmit your business message at warp speed and do it at no cost to you!

Discussion boards, blogs, e-mail lists and product review web sites are the conversations that consumers have with each other and represent the biggest collection of word-or-mouth or buzz advertising that's ever existed.

The Buzz About The Buzz

Producers of products and services are slowly starting to recognize that what Consumer reports say about their products and services isn't nearly as crucial as what consumers say to each other about them. Therefore, we have the ballooning of viral marketing…..word-of-mouth…or buzz.

And… We'll take 2 case studies as concrete proof. MSN Hotmail's viral marketing success tale is practically in the domain of folk lore. Back in 95, when Sabeer Bhatia and Jack Smith approached the venture capital firm of Draper Fisher & Jervetson with their thought for a free e-mail service, the firm liked the theme but wondered how they'd draw in members and build a company around it. Nowadays there are more than thirty million participating members.

The Hotmail user base developed faster than any media company in history; faster than CNN and AOL! Hotmail tripled its size in a single year. The present sign-up rate for new memberships frequently exceeds a 1000000 per week.

Tom Draper is the one who really suggested that they ought to append an ad message to each outbound e-mail: "P.S. Get your free email at Hotmail" and called it viral marketing.

It was a really bold move at the time. Would users resist having this automatic addition to the content of their private messages? Hotmail seasoned the idea by clearly marking the promotional plug and taking out the "P.S.".

Yet, every departing message conveyed an ad and a subtle implied endorsement by the sender. The recipient recognized that the sender was a Hotmail user and that this new free of charge e-mail thing seemed to work for them. Every new user became a 'salesman' and the content spread like an exceedingly contagious virus.

At the end of the day, Hotmail's formula for success is pretty easy. It delivers the qualities consumers truly want in an e-mail service: speed, dependability, and ease of use and a rich set of characteristics. And helped by the might of viral marketing, the rest as they state, is history.

The following success story involves a little communication tool you likely have in your personal computer right now.

The Little Tools

In 96, 4 Israeli men, 2 of whom didn't even finish senior high, dreamed up a communication system called ICQ (I Seek YOU).

After their ground forces service, the 4 men took jobs at a local PC store. At night, they worked at their dream project….a program for blink of an eye easy net communication. They named their company Mirabilis.

Net service was really expensive in Israel, so the men moved to California and later to Greater New York. It took less than eighteen months for more than ten million PC users to download and install ICQ. ICQ was free of charge.

Those ten million individuals had heard about ICQ by "word-of-mouse" advertisement. (What we call Viral marketing or Buzz marketing). Mirabilis stated a solid 'NO" to Microsoft, but accepted a three hundred million dollar take over from AOL. ICQ then swiftly exploded to 100-million downloads and a 1000000 fresh subscribers every week.

The interesting principle about ICQ is their marketing. They simply didn't do any marketing. All of their efforts were directed at inspiring users to spread the word.

One Way To Do It

They made it simple to spread the word by utilizing the standard e-mail that will ask your friends to join, but the software may likewise be instructed to scan your address book and send all your acquaintances invitation letters. Their thought was to construct a tool that includes an inherent mechanism for circulating the work and then simply letting it grow!

Now, to the meat and potatoes – You might not produce a program like hotmail or ICQ but your products may go viral, bringing in tons of subscribers and revenue.

Fasten your seatbelts as you're about to learn how. How may e-books be utilized as a tool for viral marketing? Let's suppose that you sell products utilized in baking. If on your site you provide a free of charge download of an e-book with recipes that require ingredients you sell, it's conceivable that you'll sell more of the products that you manufacture. That's the primary concept but there are a lot of ways that e-books may help acquire free viral marketing for you.

If the free of charge e-book you give away on your web site is great, informative, funny, or incorporates timely info, the public will pass that info along to their friends and loved ones and thereby, yield a lot more traffic on your web site.

The cost of an e-book is just about zilch, which makes it a pretty magnetic tool for marketers big and small. The only cost is in time and creative thinking and the advantages are endless.

Naturally, e-books don't have to be exempt. They may likewise be sold. The trick to selling your e-books is to be sure that they're worth the price you charge for them.

Many e-books now come in PDF format, as you are able to really easily and quickly convert a text document to the PDF format. The document need not be produced in HTML first.

You are able to have images and hyperlinks to web pages in a PDF e-book. Among the greatest benefits is that the PDF format may be read by both windows and MAC users.

In the next chapter you'll learn how to utilize your e-mails to produce a viral machine that steamrolls over the rivalry!

Utilizing Your Emails

Everybody wishes his or her marketing message to be viral, or have a viral facet and make the best of viral marketing. Why not? It's free of charge and effective. The issue is that most individuals don't comprehend what it is that makes their marketing e-mail message worthy of being passed along.

The idea of building an ad in email become viral is really pretty simple. You place something in there that individuals will wish to share with their loved ones and acquaintances, something they'll wish to spread around.

About Your Mail

The messages have to be perceived as having value. Crucial or timely info, research or studies are illustrations of content that might be viewed as likely pass-along stuff. Interaction content like quizzes or personality tests are things that do get passed along, as they're entertaining.

Multimedia experiences get passed along. Rich media e-mail is getting a lot of press of late. Individuals, me included, are forever touting the advantages. Yes, it does require a bit more time and revenue investment but the messages have a excellent appeal and they do get shared with other people....which is the aim of viral advertising.

Relevant info, research, or studies are all instances of content that might be viewed as possible pass-along stuff. Interaction material like a quiz or test can motivate a recipient to forward an e-mail… particularly if it is fun.

Getting recipients of your viral advertising e-mail to send it on to their acquaintances and colleagues isn't as difficult as it sounds.

The whole trick is to make them wish to share it and thereby share your ad.

Word of advice: regardless how superb you craft the offer and regardless how great the message, if the buyer visits your web site and has an experience less than what was promised, it will return to bite you. Among the greatest things about the net is that individuals who are interested in a specific subject may come together in one tiny corner of it to share ideas and info and product reviews with each other as a niche community.

Your site has to have excellent content that's centered directly at these niche markets. Rather than selling to the masses, you sell to the individuals who are thirsty for info and resources concerning their particular interest and are most likely to buy your products or services.

To achieve this, you have to identify yourself as an authority in the field you're targeting. How does one accomplish that, you might ask.

Well, the way you prove your expertise online is by putting up on your internet site with great original and useful content.

The net delivers pictures, music and video…we all recognize that…but the most effective way to lend information is, always has been and always will be, text.

Consequently, articles are the most beneficial vehicle. If you are a great author, then you have it made…if you aren't an excellent writer, there's still a way to accomplish the goal.

There are a lot of excellent places to discover content online to add to your site and you are able to get the material free, which makes it even better. For instance, article directories. The articles are free for the taking with a condition that if you display one on your site, you have to likewise cite the article's writer and link to his or her site.

Next, I'll be talking about how to make your viral niches fruitful.

Practical Ways to Go Viral

When you're seeking excellent content for your niche site, you're commonly seeking articles that are well-written and bear timely info.

The 1st option, as brought up earlier, is the article directories. The articles are free of charge but you're required to link your web site to the author's web site. So 'free of charge' isn't precisely free of charge.

The 2nd option: You want articles ghost-written for you and the way to get them is to go to article brokers. Google "Niche Article Brokers" and you'll get a lot of hits.

These companies deal with private label articles. It's content that you are able to claim as your own as all rights to the article have been sold by the writer. Now, instead of advertising somebody else as the authority, you've just demonstrated to your buyers that you, yourself, are the learned one!

You wish to make the most of the traffic you're getting on your site. So why not see to it that each visitor to your site is provided a free subscription to your e-zine within moments of getting in?

Some Tips

E-zines are a perfect illustration of informational marketing. You're presenting something of value for nothing. That value may be hard-to-find knowledge or it may be yourself.

A compelling e-zine offer matched with a easy "pass it on" technique like this won't only allow you to squeeze the most value out of each visitor to your site, but likewise give you an opt-in list of targeted leads ready and waiting to buy from you!

One of the successful attributes of a site is to maintain an e-zine by which you are able to keep in contact with your web visitors in order to maintain a reliable and long-term relationship with them through your regular e-mail to that opt-in subscriber base.

Next up, you'll discover an engaging and fun way to reach out to individuals utilizing one of the most unlikely tools around: Games.

If you've ever obtained an e-mail from a acquaintance with a link to an interesting or intriguing game, you're part of the growing target list for viral games, an net marketing tool which counts on users sending a URL to others in order to promote and theme, product or company.

Viral movies or images may be great and really funny but individuals will view them once or twice and that's it. If you are able to discover a concept that's easy to grasp, make it enjoyable and incredibly simple to utilize and then get your user to keep returning for more, you'll have the chance of exposing them a greater number of times to your message.

If you are able to add something as easy as keeping score to make a game competitive you are able to get individuals to play again and again. Offbeat games have the same effect.

The initial cost of producing a viral game is more than other viral marketing techniques but, compared to print campaigns, purchasing advertising space, radio or TV adverts, viral games are a pretty cost-efficient way of handing your market.

The other thing about games, which is difficult to put a price on, is that you are able to reach your target audience with material that's relevant and intriguing to them with ease and, once the game is set in motion, with very little work.

Although connection speed was a problem, the spread of broadband connection is slowly getting rid of that issue. There's great potential for games as a viral tool, all the same, if you're a small business, it would be best to outsource this to designers.

Viral marketing is plainly making use of the tendency of an individual to share something they find enlightening, entertaining and amazing and blogging is among the ways that viral marketing is facilitated.

These days, everyone is blogging and you are able to incorporate blogging into your sales marketing and have a lot more success.

It isn't that difficult to accomplish. Simply have your clients write diary entries about goals they've reached utilizing your product, the great emotions it's given them, the concerns and worries your product has taken out of their lives, how bad their lives were prior to them buying it, how it's helped others in their lives, how much better their lives are since they started utilizing your product, and on and on.

Clients could update their blog daily, weekly or monthly. It will hinge upon how frequently they use your product. If you're teaching them a skill, they may blog their progress.

You have to provide your buyers with web space for writing their online diary (blog) or have them e-mail you the blog entries for you to publish.

Your online blogs may be made extra persuasive by buyers including personal profiles, pictures, net video of them utilizing your product, net audio of them discussing your product, and so on.

A net blog would likely outsell the common testimonial as it's updated on a steady basis and gives more personal info and since a diary (blog) is considered private, it makes individuals more curious to read it and trust that what is said is true.

Viral and Video

Video presentations are among the most crucial tools you may develop for use in viral marketing. The reasons that a video may be so effective are many.

They're a visual tool. The vast majority of individuals are visual in the way they relate to the world around them. Even individuals who are primarily audibly oriented or kinaesthetic (sound or touch) frequently has a strong secondary visual orientation.

They're accessible. By utilizing one or two of the common formats, you may rest assured that virtually anybody will be able to view the videos.

They pack a lot of impact in a short time frame. Some of the best video promotions last no more than 30 seconds to a minute. This means there isn't much chance of the viewer losing interest before you get to your main point. That isn't always the case with a report or e-mail text.

They may be bookmarked, e-mailed as attachments, and downloaded for distribution later. Put differently, videos are easily distributed, making them ideal for sharing with others.

Movies

It's significant to note that a video that's produced as part of a viral marketing campaign is a bit different from many of the videos that proliferate around the net.

The chief purpose is to excite viewers enough that they decide they have to purchase your product or become an affiliate so they may begin making revenue with your product. There are a few matters you have to always bear in mind so your video won't become a total mess.

Many beginner video makers will inevitably make one of the following errors when producing a viral video:

Swamping the viewer with so much sensory stimulation that the message is lost underneath all the pretty extras. You need the special effects to enhance your content, not hide it.

Don't be too cute with the demonstration. Keep the cute factor to a minimum...unless you're touting an informational product on minding kittens.

Attempt to stand back from becoming a condensed infomercial. Think in terms of 30-second commercials that you've watched in years past that got right to the point and still held your attention – that's the angle you wish to go after.

Don't utilize verbiage that's likely to offend others. While this might sound like a common sense approach, it's astonishing how many sales oriented videos online today totally forget this!

Don't produce something that will be dated in a year's time. The fact is that when a video recording goes viral, it's out there broadcasting from now on. If you rely to a great extent on cultural benchmarks that are clearly an denotation of a specific time era, you run the risk of turning individuals off as they believe the video is old and the product is likely old and outdated.

Don't release a video till you're totally happy with it. Remember that the video represents you and your product. If you've doubts about the calibre or the structure of the video, there's a great chance that other people will feel the same way.

When you've your concept, your primary script and a great idea of how to stage the action for the video recording, you're ready to start the actual digital filming.

Essentially, you've 2 options open to you when things get to this stage. Either you may do it yourself or you may have the video assembled by a pro. There are a few pros and cons to both approaches that you ought to consider.

A lot of entrepreneurs decide to assemble their own viral marketing videos. And many of these videos do work all right and generate plenty of positive attention, resulting in traffic and sales.

The benefits to doing the video yourself being you get low production costs, you don't have to be technically disposed thanks to technological gains and you may change things at the last moment.

But you might face issues of poor visual quality, sub-par gear and the whole video might obviously look amateurish.

Going with a pro to produce your video may be the best option in some cases. There are several advantages to having the video assembled by a pro.

After all, with their expertise and high-end tools, you'll receive slick production quality, the output in several formats and access to tools you don't have.

However in the flip side, the video will cost a bit, last moment changes are hard or even impossible to make, you lose a particular amount of originate control and still have to pay even if you don't like the final product!

Your Own Viral Video Show

As more and more markets get receptive to the application of viral marketing techniques, the viral video recording has continued to evolve and adjust to more settings. There are a lot of reasons why videos take off so well as viral tools. A few good reasons one may think of are:

The subject matter adds up to the viewers. There's immediate rapport accomplished that allows viewers to comprehend and relate to what is going on in the video recording.

The video recording is simple to download and easier to distribute. While often individuals will share a link to the video recording, they might also wish to download it. The video ought to be uploaded and distributed to popular video sites like youtube.com, or Google video.

The logical conclusion of the video motivates a "wow" factor. That is, by the time viewers reach the end of the video, they're already sold on the need for the product and are open to finding out how to acquire it. At the same time, they've already thought of a few individuals who need to see the video recording and make plans to pass the word along.

Types Of Video

The 3 types of videos that commonly draw attention are the entertaining viral video, the informational viral video recording and the conversational viral video.

Occasionally you might wish to go the comedic or satirical way. Occasionally the informational style works very well in settings where a direct approach is anticipated. Illustration: marketing an informational product that has to do with a serious subject.

Conversational styles frequently include utilizing testimonials related to how the product helped individuals, and frequently looks as if everybody were standing around having a casual conversation.

Now we're going to discuss Ustream.tv. And this is essentially a site where you are able to produce your own live video show. And what's

Excellent about Ustream is that it's free to set up and it's a different viral marketing tool that may just drive swarms of traffic to your business, and it's really easy to get doing. All you require is a basic web cam which most laptops come preinstalled with a web cam.

So you go over to Ustream.tv, you're merely going to click on sign up to get rolling, and you simply produce your new account, fill in that

Info and you'll going to get an e-mail sent to you with details. After that, login to your Ustream account.

And what you are going to do when you login is you're going to see an selection that says 'my shows' and you may click on that and you can name a new show, illustration: test Ustream show.

So if it's travelling, you'll put up whatever subject that is. If its news sports, entertainment, business, applied science, and so forth. Or you may plug in your own text. Ustream is a really high traffic site. And, you are able to likewise schedule your posts here; you can simply follow all the on-screen instructions. And when you're finished, you simply click on "save changes" and your test show will be live.

What makes the service particularly useful as well is that it blends live and archived footage seamlessly. Users may watch a show as its occurring, or only return and watch shows after they're off the air. The player may be embedded on third-party sites or sent to more than twenty social networks, and the service has likewise introduced an iPhone app. The free app lets you watch live and pre-recorded UStream material, search and browse through the library of shows, and chat with other users.

Along with its public-facing product, UStream likewise powers a private-label service known as Watershed. This service lets groups customize, in both look and feel, and limit the distribution to picked out users. The UStream interface is clean and aboveboard. It offers an easy option for broadcasting your own videos or checking out others', and at no cost to you.

And then what's going to occur is you're going to begin acquiring more followers and the whole video snowballs into a monolithic viral campaign in double quick time.

Tagging and Scripts

A Fresh consumer phenomenon is known as "tagging" or "folksonomies" (short for folks and taxonomy). Tagging is mighty because consumers are producing an organizational structure for net content. Folksonomies not only enable individuals to file away content under tags, but, even greater, share it with other people by filing it under a global taxonomy that they produced.

Some Tricks

Here's how tagging works: utilizing sites such as del.icio.us - a bookmark sharing web site – and Flickr - a photograph sharing web site - consumers are getting together on categorizing net content under particular keywords, or tags.

For example, a person may post photos of their iPod on Flickr and file it under the tag "iPod". These pictures are now not only visible

Below the individual user's iPod tag but likewise under the community iPod tag that shows all images consumers are rendering and filing under the keyword.

Tagging is catching on, as it's a natural complement to search. Type the word "blogs" into Google and it can't tell if you're searching for info about how to launch a blog, how to read blogs, or anything else.

While tags are far from perfect, marketers ought to, all the same, be utilizing them to keep a finger on the pulse of the general public.

Begin subscribing to RSS feeds to monitor how consumers are tagging info related to your product, service, and company or web space. These are living focus groups that are available free of charge, day in and day out.

One technique of viral marketing is utilizing tell-a-friend script on your site. This is a simple computer programming script that you are able to attach to the programming on your web site.

Commonly tell a friend scripts are installed in pages where media is posted so that an individual may easily send the media to any of his acquaintances or loved ones and accomplish it swiftly.

Essentially the tell a friend script is a script where a individual may input his name, e-mail address, the recipient's e-mail address and send off the media to his acquaintance or loved ones much like an e-mail with an attachment.

Once the recipient gets the e-mail, he won't think of it as spam mail as he sees the senders name as somebody he recognizes and trusts.

Once the e-mail is opened, it will be read, watched or played. Included in the e-mail would be a short description of the company or web site that sponsors the media sent and a different tell a friend script. Then the procedure starts once more.

Tell a friend script is really easy and does not require a complicated method of programming. You'll be able to simply copy and paste a script and merely put it on a designated page.

Utilize your favourite search engine and type in "tell a friend script". There will be a lot of results. There are free of charge ones and paid ones. You simply utilize the one that best fits your needs.

By utilizing tell a friend script, you are able to possibly drive traffic into your web site and that may spell profits.

Discussion Boards and Forums

Recently, discussion board marketing has been touted as a sort of free, organic, viral marketing. Nevertheless, because so many marketers go into discussion boards purely with the aim of marketing products or services, their actions and attitude inadvertently induces the exact opposite of the desired effect.

Know This

Discussion boards aren't marketplaces but when utilized as such, the marketers' actions become offensive and will only prompt the wrath of fellow members and marketers, let alone moderators who may ban them from the web site.

In order to be effective, this sort of marketing carries a particular degree of dedication, responsibility and respect. The beginning requirement is to take a personal interest in the chief subject of the discussion board.

Not only does that imply visiting it on a regular basis, but it likewise implies developing a great relationship with both other members and the moderators, as well as taking an active interest in assisting other people.

Naturally, it likewise implies following and all rules that exist. By doing this, one may develop a reputation and, since its human nature to work with a trusted colleague, business will of course develop from this.

Here are some tips to effectively use forum marketing as a part of your overall net marketing strategy.

Find the correct discussion boards:

Not all bulletin boards are worth your time. Seek popular forums that cover your niche topic. Begin by asking your employees, suppliers, and buyers which net communities they hang out in. Likewise, try searching discussion board hub sites like Board Reader, Big Boards, and Board Tracker using niche-specific keywords.

Narrow your list to 5-10 that will be worth your time utilizing the following criteria:

• Seek discussion boards that have at least 1,000 members and 10,000 posts.

• Make certain the discussion board gets at least 10 to 15 new posts on a daily basis.

• Discount discussion boards that are overrun by spam.

• Avoid discussion boards hosted by your direct competitors.

Check the user agreement and posting guideposts:

During the registration procedure, you'll be asked to agree to the forum's user agreement and posting guideposts. Study these carefully. There's a lot of boilerplate legal language in these documents, so it's tempting to just skip them without reading. But, many discussion boards have unique guidelines that you have to pay attention to. Some of the most crucial to look for include:

• Are users allowed to put links in their posts?

• Are users allowed to market their own businesses?

• Are users allowed to post commercial messages in their signatures?

Create a compelling profile:

A great profile may help you establish credibility on the discussion board. Provide a solid description of your expertise and experience. Feel free to add in a few personal titbits to humanize your profile. Stay away from sharing possibly polarizing data like political or religious affiliation. Supply contact info so other users may get in touch with you if they're interested in learning more about your business.

Introduce yourself:

Many forums encourage fresh users to introduce themselves to the community by making an introductory post. This is commonly done in threads particularly designated for welcoming fresh members. Your introductory post ought to include a short description of your expertise and an explanation of how come you joined the forum. Don't make any marketing pitches in your 1st post. If you try to sell anything in your 1st post, you'll very likely get banned.

Spend some time loitering:

Resist the urge to begin posting immediately. Discussion boards are tight-knit communities that tend to shun and haze newbies. Spend a little time reading the forum to get a sense of the community's particular quirks and cultural norms.

Place your site address in your signature:

Discussion board signatures are blocks of text or graphic that is attached to the end of all your posts. Most individuals use signatures to display their favourite quotes or links to their favourite sites. Some discussion boards also let users to utilize signatures to promote their own sites. If you're in a discussion board that allows self-promotional signatures, make certain you take full advantage of this opportunity.

Stand back from drama:

Don't get drawn into heated arguments. It would be a shame to get banned simply because you began arguing. Here's how you may avoid the drama:

• Perpetually remind yourself that your mission here is to establish good will for your business.

• Stand back from charged subjects like politics or religion.

• Withstand the urge to respond to critique. If you have to answer, at least give yourself a few hours to cool off before reacting.

• Utilize emoticons to indicate when you're being facetious.

• End discussions the minute you sense that it's getting contentious. Simply say you agree to disagree and that you wish to move on to other more pleasant topics.

Once you've the respect of the users, you may begin more aggressive marketing campaigns. Centre on marketing strategies that provide an advantage for the forum community. For instance, offer the forum members special discounts, free of charge samples, or fun contests. Make sure to get the permission of the forum's moderators before you begin these campaigns.

This sort of marketing has already suffered a little abuse and because of this, a lot of discussion boards have recently developed rigorous rules designed to protect their members from abusive or overly-aggressive marketing manoeuvres.

Marketers have to respect that the purpose of a discussion board is to be a platform to exchange thoughts on a given subject. By centering on the subject and posting inquiries and answers, a marketer's reputation will grow and this produces the potential for sales by nature.

Wrapping it up

You've just seen the most often utilized viral techniques by most marketers in producing a successful and viral web campaign.

All you have to do is be creative and think out of the box. In doing so, you are able to think of so many additional ways to get your viral message going and going.

A few matters you need to bear in mind when producing a successful viral product:

Material:

The success of any viral marketing and web campaign is directly related to the material of the viral message by whatever vehicle it's delivered, be it, e-mail, e-zines, sites, etc. Really great, creative, and inspired material may and does bring in buyers by the numbers. Illustrations include valuable discounts, relevant data, jokes and multimedia goodies. User

Satisfaction:

Viral and web marketing efforts may provide enormous advantages to e-commerce sites by bringing in fresh users but most fail to totally appreciate the promotional advantages of user satisfaction. Viral marketing is a two-way street. The news that your e-business didn't provide as promised travels like a racing bullet and twice as fast as the speed of light.

Trust:

Trust is the all-important lubricant of Web business; without trust, business grates to a halt and establishing trust takes time and work on your part. It isn't something that buyers give freely. You have to earn it and continue to earn it with each sale.

Well, I wish you the best for your viral and web campaigns, but in whatever medium you pick out, forever remember the above 3 factors.

Tips for Success

To succeed through live video, the secret is yet again to provide value as information and entertainment. But at the same time, it's to use other social media platforms to generate hype and buzz for your event – start promoting your live streaming event early on and find ways to engage your audience by inviting them to participate in various ways where applicable.

This is also great for tying together with competitions and other types of time-sensitive marketing. Think too about things that benefit from being live.

concerts, travel, interviews and more all feel a lot more exciting when live.

How about a live launch event for your product? Likewise, how about letting your viewers send in live questions, something that can be exciting and give them direct access to your brand. Make sure that your audience feel.

as though they're getting live, unrestricted access to something exciting and different and you'll be able to generate excitement.

And if you're not quite ready to go live in front of the camera yet, consider using other live 'events' for your marketing. This could mean a Reddit AMA (Ask Me Anything) or a Google Hangout.

That's a lot of information we've covered and a lot of different strategies. We've seen how to set up a social media empire and how to thrive across all platforms and on certain platforms specifically. We've looked at how to leverage new emerging technologies, we've seen apps and tools you can use and we've addressed the psychology of sharing.

But throughout all of this, what has remained the most important is that you deliver value. Value is what draws people to any social media account, just as it's what draws them to a website. Value is what keeps them there and it's what keeps them clicking on your links and sharing your posts.

And moreover, value is what helps you to build your reputation as a brand that can deliver. And this is absolutely crucial – because there's no point having a big audience if that audience doesn't trust you and isn't interested in what you have to offer. Don't post clickbait or spam the web with promotional messages – use your social media accounts to show what's important to your organization, to entertain your visitors and to show that you know your topic inside out.

Likewise, make sure that you are actually engaging with the audience that visit your site. Respond to comments, ask questions and contribute to the communities you join. This way people will feel like they know you and they'll go from being customers and leads to being fans and real contacts. Every single one of those followers can be turned into a fan and 1,000 true fans is really all any business needs to go nuclear.

The key then is truly to just think carefully about what you post and to hold yourself to high standards. Think about how you want to be seen on social media and about what impression you want to make. If you do this, then you'll find that you attract new followers and new customers like a magnet. Social media is like a megaphone and will amplify your message. This can be irritating, or it can be a great way to demonstrate your enthusiasm and passion to the masses.

Erin Lovett, has 12 years industry experience in internet marketing and web research.

This Book "SHow to go Viral in The Marketing World" shows her in-depth tips,tactics of social media marketing strategies, to enhance your business and dominate the social media!

GOOD LUCK!

www.ingramcontent.com/pod-product-compliance
Lightning Source LLC
Chambersburg PA
CBHW050912180526
45159CB00007B/2888

9781537461991